SAECULUM

Sean Colletti

BARE FICTION
POETRY

First published in Great Britain by
Bare Fiction
177 Copthorne Road,
Shrewsbury SY3 8NA
www.barefictionmagazine.co.uk

Bare Fiction. Reg. No. 8798494

A CIP catalogue record of this book is available from the British Library.

ISBN: 978-1-910896-13-6

Edited by Robert Harper
Cover image by Hannah Swingler
Cover design by Robert Harper

Printed and bound in Poland by BooksFactory.co.uk

for Jes & Anne

Before figuring out whether or not
it is ironic to not know the meaning
of onomastics and having to search
etymology of names, I decide to exhale.

There is a football on the outside
of the pitch, rolling in dirt and grass
away from my course trajectory,
and I wonder which of your instincts

would kick in: the embarrassment
of your weak arms or your maternal
impulse of wanting to care for every
concentration of organic matter.

My name means something like
God's gift, but no one ever told me
which god. I came across you in
Hesiod once. Maybe I'm there, too.

I was never good at giving presents,
so I built you a model of an atom
and said "This is how I picture us."
I think you took that to mean we
were the protons and neutrons in
the nucleus, which would have been
the kind of premise to a film
we never would have watched.
But what I actually meant was you
were the proton and I was the
electron, pacing back and forth—
waiting for you to respond to me
in any way. I guess when an atom
splits, it's a kind of response.

***

You are whatever I want you to be.
Nowadays, you are "Collapse the Light
Into Earth" by Porcupine Tree. Not
the difficult, technical songs I listen to
while cleaning. The simple, quiet ones.
I fit you in where you don't belong and
ignore every lyric that contradicts you.

What I miss about the sex
are the DVD title screens
on loop in the background.
No one watches DVDs anymore.

When you're with your husband
now, do you pause before the next
episode loads? Or have you seen these all
before? At a certain point, does
Netflix ask if you're still watching?

$$***$$

The Radisson at the center of the universe
has a cocktail bar that serves all night.
I go in at four o'clock and notice there's not
even a bell for last call. You are somewhere
on the twenty-seventh floor at a party
out of *Eyes Wide Shut*. I am reading a menu
that says they use Talisker in their Old
Fashioneds; I might be here a while. Besides,
we both know you're just going to make fun
of how my double t's sound like d's, and I
am going to pretend like it bothers me.

7

When I met you, I cracked open
your skull and spray-painted
the sides of your cerebellum:
STOP BEING SO NICE!

I forgot to close you back up,
so it shows like a tattoo; but
you have always been the kind
of person to care more about
the aesthetics than the meaning.
I have never been able to empathize.

When I met you, you reached into
your chest, and your presentation
reminded me of the critically-
panned *DragonHeart*. I never
told you this, because I didn't
think you would understand.

I still listen to Randy Edelman's
"To the Stars" and cry. You forgot
to close yourself back up, and I don't
know what to do with this anymore.

When you checked me out,
you skipped the introduction
but—otherwise—read cover
to cover. When I checked you
out, I looked at the names and
dates on the card in the front
to see where and when you'd been.

There should be a word for the condition
that makes me blurt out words when I'm
thinking about something embarrassing.
It's never quite a full sentence or phrase,
even, and I always try to pass it off as
clearing my throat or humming a tune.
Maybe the word could be onomatopoetic—
something like Bribratwhum Syndrome.
The other day, I was thinking about our
picnic in the park—how the tea was cold
by the time we found somewhere to sit
and how I kissed you with my eyes open to
see if anyone was watching us—and I came
down with a case of the bribratwhums.

You spread out tarot cards on the carpet in front of us and—as you try explaining the meaning of things you don't actually know—all I can think about is how hard it has become for me to sit cross-legged for more than a few minutes. "Did you know The Tower means you're not as stable as you think you are?" you ask. "Did *you* know one can get pins and needles in one's testicles?" I want to respond. I keep waiting for your phone to buzz or for you to remember something on the desk you need so that I can check to see if I'm still here.

What bothered me wasn't the embarrassment
of fumbling with the condom or not being able
to keep it up. It was how—when you sat there
afterwards, enjoying the cold and the light on
the spiderwebs under the awning—you didn't
care there was an opossum watching us.

***

No one asked who you were when you
picked me up from karaoke, and I'm
beginning to think it was because they
knew. If you had arrived any earlier,
you might have seen me do "Breakdown"
by Tom Petty and the Heartbreakers.
If you had arrived any later, you might
have seen me and decided to go home.

Tear up the carpet
by your wall heater.
The fabric's split

ends are still bent
down, and it's time
you find something new.

Hurry, while the stores
are still open. They say
smell is the most powerful

sense in bringing back
memories, but I dare you
to lie down there and feel.

You could bubble wrap
and mail it first class, but
standard shipping is fine.

There is a patch of floor
by the side of my bed
that needs replacing—

the first and last place
on which I stand
before I wake and sleep.

I have found the perfect leaf on which to sit
and pretend like I'm doing work, chewing loudly.
I meditate so I can feel every part of my exoskeleton.
You land opposite with two offspring, and they
begin tearing up my leaf. I blink a glossy blink
trying to tell you to get them under control,
but you twitch your wings to show them how to
fly. I'd like to join, but I keep pretending to work.

***

There should be a word for when friends
break up. Maybe it could change depending
on how important each friendship was.

Mike might have had an easy dent up
with Steve. Alex knew Lily a bit longer, so their
crack up was more noticeable to their families.

I wouldn't call what we went through a
shatter up, but that's only because when I
see you, you look so well put-together.

We rehearse our parting
like a stage performance

or farewell tour, where we
play all our greatest hits from

memory. We allow ourselves
one cover song but disagree

on which Radiohead closer,
because you like *Amnesiac*

more than anyone should.
Have you even listened to

the version of "Videotape"
that's on *From the Basement?*

When the show is over and
the audience congratulates us,

I play an encore in my head:
you sitting across from me with

a bottle of Mexican beer and a
hand occasionally covering a smile.

We follow one another backstage,
our teeth bouncing off each other.

When I went in for corrective nostalgia,
the nurse had me fill out forms about which
memories to target and how I wanted to feel
differently about them. I asked to
hate high school, so I could fit in with
everyone else. I made a list of every
parenting choice my mom and dad
improvised and requested that the doctor
make them all wrong in retrospect
so I would have more to write about.

For each memory of you, I wrote how I
wanted them to stay the same but with
very specific background music and a
slightly darker hue that had the added
synesthesia of smelling like recent rain.

***

Her birthday happened to fall on a Thursday
that year and was never able to get back up.

She spends a different day each year reaching
for some spot on her head, like a phantom limb;

the smell of wax and smoke
coming from somewhere.

I hated our .mp3 lives,
always trying to present the
best parts of ourselves, as if
filler sections were shameful.
What I would have given to
turn us into the wheels of a
cassette tape—Tom Petty's
Wildflowers—so we could wrap
around each other
from beginning to end
without skipping tracks.
You could have shown me
your "Don't Fade on Me"
and I could have shown
you my "Wake Up Time",
one side coming to an end
as the other side begins.

***

Matter cannot be created or destroyed
and liquids conform to the shapes of their

containers, so I pour you into a
cup and watch you evaporate.

A tanker is carrying quicklime and hits a lamppost in Ashfield
at 7:00 p.m. You are watching TV in Ashfield. It is 7:00 p.m.

Quicklime. Freshman biology slides off the tight-
ropes of your synapses like sand. Quicksand.

You are no longer in Ashfield. You are in a pit of limes, sinking.
You are yelling at the Golden Retriever, but she is licking herself.

You are almost completely submerged. You are terrified
that quicklime might have nothing to do with biology.

There is no Wikipedia at the bottom of this pit.
There is no wireless signal. There is no...

A procession of cars
diverted by roadwork
foots along this street
it has never seen
and is unlikely to see
ever again. I stare out
the screen door the same
way I did out tinted
car windows when I
was growing up here.
Not only can they not
see me—they cannot see
the palm fronds covering
the pavement on windy
days, they cannot feel
the lost garden snake
between their toes and
they cannot hear the
echoing bounce of the
basketball at sundown.

Your parents ask you *What do you
want to be when you grow up?* You tell them
Better at naming animals than you.

You still don't know cat species
very well, but whatever Bob is, he is
unique—not always in a good way.

He has a nub of a tail, severed at
birth. He would eat nothing but bacon,
if left to his own devices. This

is what makes sleeping in on
Sundays so difficult: the frying pan
coming out of the drawer (before

the smell of fat even begins
to flood the kitchen) sends him
into a wail more than a cry.

Bob stares at walls as if listening
to an old friend. He outlives the first
round of cats—father to the second.

When he bathes them, they kick
at his face like rabbits running in place.
He waits for the anger to pass—

absorbs it in knocks to the chin—
and closes his eyes before drawing them
closer, like a Chinese finger trap.

When you wake on a Sunday morning
to the slanted light from the window shades—
when there is silence—you know.

You overhear the neighbor say she found
him in the street—that the coyotes must have
got him. But you imagine more than coyotes.

You see owls and raccoons, too, and
Bob, lying there, purring, saying *Please,*
eat of my flesh. Let none go hungry.

I first saw the cheetah sitting in front of a Greyhound station.
"Excuse me," I began to say to her, but she bit me in the leg.
One of her teeth broke off in a bone. "Why would you do that?"

"I thought you were going to ask me for money," she said.
"Well, now I have a tooth in my leg." "Sorry. You can keep it
as a memento." I did. "Why are you waiting out here?" I asked.

"I've just moved in from back east. I wanted to try my hand
at acting." I looked at her paws. "You realize how ridiculous
that sounds coming from you?" "So they say. So they say."

"Why do you want to act?" I asked after minutes of silence,
staring at her coat, the spots of which were oddly shaped
and disproportionate. "I think it would be a good way of

finding myself." I closed my umbrella and beat her
over the head with it. "Thousands of people come here
every year saying the same thing. What makes you

so special?" The cheetah growled at me. "I happen
to be classically trained and fluent in thirty different
languages." "*Bullshit*. I can spot a liar when I see one.

What talents do you *actually* possess?" She shrunk back
and said "I can run fast." "We'll see just how fast you can
run." I called my lawyer and had him bring over a contract

stating that if the cheetah beat me in a race, I would get her
an audition, but if *I* won, she was mine. The cheetah signed,
confident of herself. But, like most cheetahs, she neglected

the fine print, which stipulated that the distance of the race be thirteen miles. She ran out of breath after one minute and, when I passed her, she said that I had tricked her.

"Are you calling me a cheat-ah?" "I suppose you think that's terribly clever." After the race, I brought her home, my first companion in years. She urinated on the carpet.

That night, I heard her growling in the backyard.
She was sitting on the grass, head pointed up at
the moon. I sat beside her for an hour, listening.

"What are you doing?" I finally asked. "What
does it look like I'm doing? I'm embracing my
cultural background by barking at the moon."

"Wolves bark at the moon," I said. "Exactly."
The cheetah was so sure of herself that I didn't
want to say anything else, but it was against my

nature not to. "Cheetahs descend from cats,
not dogs." She growled a few more times, half-
heartedly, and lay down. "I thought if I really

tried and believed it, it could be true." "Well,
now you know how deists feel." I scratched
her head and the two of us stayed there all

night, telling jokes whose punch-lines were
the names of people we knew. "Do you think
we'll ever walk on the moon?" she asked me.

"That happened over forty years ago." "No,
I mean you and I. Do you think *we'll* ever
walk on the moon?" I told her I didn't know.

"I'd like to live on the moon." We stopped
making jokes and listed off everything
we wanted to do before we died, knowing

that we wouldn't do most of them. "That's
just how things go," she said. "But if I could do
just one thing…" I waited for her to finish

the thought, but she had fallen asleep. I sat
there until sunrise, watching her stomach,
trying to synchronize my breaths with hers.

The cheetah stood on the table, looking at me after the doctor left. "What did he say?" she asked. "He said to count backwards from ten, and that would be it." "But I don't know how to count to ten at all,

much less backwards." "I know." We waited. "Did I ever tell you about The Alchemist?" "I don't remember you mentioning it," I said. "The Alchemist. That is how cheetahs understand dreams. There is

an Alchemist in your head who crafts dream potions. Sometimes, they're good potions. Sometimes, they're bad. I just hope this one is good." The doctor came back in and stuck the needle in the back

of her neck. I started counting backwards, but when I reached zero, she was still looking sideways into my eyes. She was trying hard to say something, but she could barely breathe. I held her paw

until she fell over. As I walked back to the car, I tried picturing her visiting The Alchemist's shop. She bought a potion, drank it and fell asleep smiling. I sat in the car and cried for three hours.

Years later, I went to the spot in the backyard where she was buried, carrying pliers in one hand. "I know you said I should keep it as a memento, but if I can't remember you without it, then I don't

want to remember at all." I bent down and pulled the tooth out of my leg. "I can't carry you with me everywhere I go." It fell without making a sound, and I kicked dirt over it. That night,

I dreamt. The cheetah and I were walking through the snow. She said how the fact she wasn't cold was testament to her being descended from wolves. We laughed, but when I reached down to pet her, she was gone. And I was no longer walking. I was in mid-sprint, on all fours, black spots covering my forearms. I could spring forever without getting tired. When I

woke up, I had shin splints, and there was a black spot where I had pulled the tooth from my leg. I spent the rest of the day smiling, knowing that her last potion had been a good one.

I know I should have lied,
claiming I woke up and saw it
between the children crying
and the man snoring next to me
to enhance the effect somehow.

But, really, it was only by chance
that I gently lifted the eye mask
long enough to see it at the window
as we flew over the last stretch
of the Atlantic: the horizon,

composed of each color of the
rainbow, sandwiched between
a carpet of clouds and a ceiling
of nighttime sky with only a few
visible stars. In those moments,

I always felt the pressure to
experience something profound—
to reach for ephemeral evidence
that explains how each layer
of color conveniently represents

a different part of me or to
consider that the red at the
bottom made part of the cloud-
line look like it was on fire and
that was meaningful. But,

truthfully, all I was thinking
about was coming home to you
and how I always found it funny
writing palindromes as a child—
mom, dad, Bob, racecar—and,

since no one taught me the word
until later, how it felt like I
discovered palindromes myself
and they were somehow mine.
Nothing to do with sunrises, really.

You start having nightmares on a
Saturday, which is inconvenient,
because you like things to start on
Sundays. How are you supposed to
respond to your therapist when she
asks, next month, "So, how long have
you been having these nightmares?"
You'll have to say "X number of weeks…
and one day." You grind your teeth.

You come up with stories to tell
your partner to explain why you
wake up screaming: "I had a dream
that I poured a bowl of cereal, but
there was no milk" or "I had a dream
that I was on *Millionaire* and the last
question was about Scandinavian
black metal, so I won, of course" or
"I love you so much, babe, that it
scares me". You grin. She turns over
and covers her ears with a pillow.

You wait until 2:00 a.m. before you
put on a horror film as a form of protest.
If you're going to have nightmares,
you will have them your way, okay?

You feel sleep coming in advance
like a Jehovah's Witness to your door.
You breathe in for three seconds and
hold for three seconds. One: you haven't
taken your socks off yet, but you've
resigned yourself to the fact you won't.
Two: is your heart beating faster than
it should be? Remind yourself to look up
average heart rate tomorrow. Three:
maybe tonight will be different.
You breathe out for three seconds.

Acknowledgements

This pamphlet would not exist without the help, care and insight of the following people.

The editors of Bad Betty Press and *Ink, Sweat & Tears*, for publishing two of these pieces in their original forms under the titles "On Sleep" and "Quicklime".

My greatest teachers in the classroom: Randy Cox, Christina Pages, Renny Christopher, Sean Carswell, Gillian Wright, Hugh Adlington, Richard House, Elsa Braekkan Payne and Luke Kennard.

My greatest teachers outside of the classroom: Bohdan Piasecki, Leon Priestnall, Toby Campion, Vanessa Kisuule and especially my editor, Robert Harper.

Those who have gone out of their way to champion my work to others: Gary Longden, Jo Bell, Joelle Taylor and Stuart Bartholomew.

Writers' Bloc (past and present) and the UniSlam and Birmingham poetry communities.

My teammates: Tom Crossland, Daisy Edwards, Jake Scott, Anne Gill, Hannah Ledlie, Tian Sewell-Morgan, Kieran Hayes, Mikey Barnes, Kimberley Knaggs and Hannah Swingler.

My friends and family from California (some of whom have also moved away), but especially my parents and brother.

Additional thanks to: Luke Kennard, for reading this pamphlet in advance and providing his overly-generous words; Hannah Swingler, for designing the cover image; Anne Gill, for making each day worth living.

And, always, Jes: I wish you were here to read this.